Title: "Journey into Electricity and Automation

In the picturesque town of Naples, where the gentle hum of nature met the occasional buzz of technology, lived a young and inquisitive engineer named Frank. He had always been captivated by the magic of electricity, the invisible force that powered the world around him. One day, as he gazed out at the rolling hills that surrounded his home, a spark of curiosity ignited within him, setting him on a journey to unravel the mysteries of circuits and current

CONTENT:

Title: "Journey into Electricity and Automation 1

Chapter 1: The Essence of Electricity 4

Chapter 2: The Dance of Electrons 6

Chapter 3: Navigating Circuits 7

CHAPTER 4: WIRES AND CONDUCTORS 9

chapter 5: Ohm's Law and Beyond 11

Chapter 6: Series, Parallel, and Complex Circuits 13

Chapter 7: Applications and Innovations 15

Chapter 8: The Power of Knowledge and Imagination through automation 16

Epilogue: 18

CHAPTER 9: SHORT STORIES   20

1) "LILLY'S QUEST FOR ELECTRICAL KNOWLEGE" 21

2) "The Electric Revolution" 26

3) "The Rise of Automation" 29

4) "Sparks of Innovation" 32

5) "ALEX AND THE TRADE SCHOOL" 36

6) "SARA AND THE MECHANICS" 40

7) Title: The Symphony of Process Control 42

Franks story: 47

Chapter 1: The Essence of Electricity

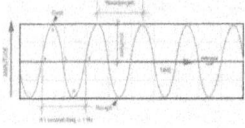

Franks quest for knowledge began with a fundamental question: What is electricity? Through his studies, he came to understand that electricity is the flow of electrons through a conductor, carrying energy from one point to another. This realization opened up a world of possibilities and sparked his imagination. Frank discovered that there are 2 forms of electricity, A/C which is alternating current. He found that in an A/C circuit the current changes direction every cycle. He found that there are 60 cycles in one second and that the cycles are called Hertz. In a typical sign wave the voltage reverses direction 60 times every second and so does the current.

Chapter 2: The Dance of Electrons

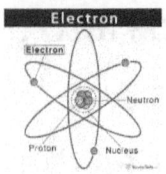

Delving deeper into the realm of electrons, Frank learned about the structure of atoms and the role of electrons in creating electric current. He marveled at the intricate dance of these tiny particles and how their movements could power the devices that defined modern life. This is how electric current, or amperage, is produced. An ampere (A) is the standard unit of electric current in the International System of Units (SI), representing the steady current produced by one volt driving a one-ohm resistance. A coulomb (C) quantifies electric charge, equivalent to the charge transported by a current of one ampere in one second. Amperes measures the flow rate of electric charge, analogous to water flow in a river. In contrast, coulombs measure the total quantity of electricity, similar to the volume of water in a container. Amperes are used in practical applications like determining the capacity of electrical wires and safety devices.

Coulombs are used in contexts like battery capacities and electrostatic experiments. If we measure the electrons passing by one point in one second, we will read $$I = \frac{Q}{t}$$

Where:
- (I) represents the current in amperes.
- (Q) denotes the charge in coulombs.
- (t) is the time in seconds.

But in the electrical world this is impractical, and we would just use an amp meter.

Chapter 3: Navigating Circuits

As Frank ventured further into his exploration, he encountered the concept of circuits. He discovered that a circuit is a closed loop through which electricity can flow, connecting various components to form a functional system. Through hands-on experiments and tinkering with circuit diagrams, Frank learned how to navigate the pathways of current flow. He found that there are series circuits, parallel circuits and a combo of series, parallel circuits. Each circuit has its own set of math rules for discovering total resistance, total current and applied voltage as well as total power in watts.

CHAPTER 4: WIRES AND CONDUCTORS

In his pursuit of understanding, Frank explored the properties of conductors and insulators. He discovered that conductors, such as copper and aluminum, allow electricity to flow freely, while insulators, like rubber and plastic, block the flow of electrons. Armed with this knowledge, Frank experimented with dissimilar materials to observe their conductive properties. Copper wire is the best conductor for electricity. There is a voltage drop formula

The formula for calculating voltage drop in an AC circuit is: Single phase voltage drop formula: $2 \times K \times I \times D / KCMIL$. Three phase voltage drop formula: $1.73 \times K \times I \times D / KCMIL$

- (K) Direct current constant (12.9 for copper and 21.2 for aluminum)
- (I) Denotes current in amps
- (D) denotes distance
- (CM) is circular mills

Example: For a length of 160 feet of number 6 copper wire drawing a current of 44 amps at a voltage of 240 vac

2 x 12.9 x 44 x 160 = 181632 / 26240 = 6.92
Voltage drop = 6.92
Working voltage = 240 – 6.92 = 233.08 vac
Voltage drop = 2.9 %

A voltage drop of 3% is preferred in all wiring design applications

chapter 5: Ohm's Law and Beyond

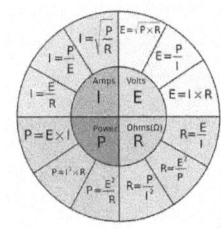

Equipped with a deeper understanding of electrical fundamentals, Frank delved into Ohm's Law and its implications for circuit analysis. He found that a scientist by the name of Ohm produced a set of rules for figuring out circuits. He explored the mathematical relationships between voltage, current, and resistance, gaining insights into how changes in one parameter affected the others. Through problem-solving scenarios and real-world applications, Frank honed his ability to predict and control electrical behavior.

He looked up the basic formulas for OHMS Law:

E = Voltage

I = amperage or intensity

R = resistance

W = Watts

E = I X R

R = E/I

I = E/R

W = P X E

Frank discovered that another scientist by the name of Kirchoff produced another set of laws for parallel circuits for figuring out current.

Chapter 6: Series, Parallel, and Complex Circuits

As Frank journey progressed, he encountered the intricacies of series, parallel, and complex circuits. He experimented with different circuit configurations, observing how components were connected and how current flowed through each path. Through trial and error, Frank mastered the art of designing circuits that met specific requirements and optimized performance. He also learned that resistance plays a big part in a circuit and that series circuits have different rules than parallel circuits. In a series circuit the current is the same for the entire circuit, but the voltage drops across each resistor, and the sum of the voltage drops equals the applies voltage. To get total circuit resistance just add all the resistors.

In a parallel circuit the voltage is the same across all resisters but the current divides, and the circuit total resistance is smaller than the largest resistor.

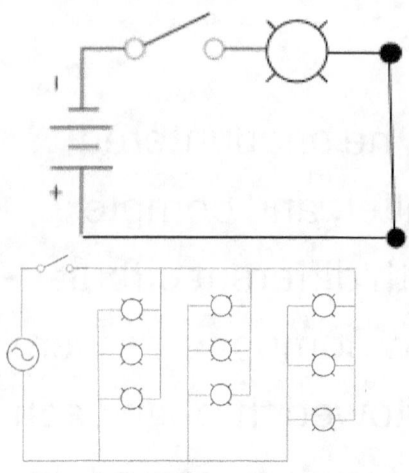

Simple lighting series circuit

Simple Parallel lighting circuit

I=E/Rt

I=E/Rt

Rt= R1+R2+R3...

Rt= 1/(1/R1 + 1/R2 + 1/R3...)

Simple circuit with a 3-way switch

Chapter 7: Applications and Innovations

In the final stretch of his odyssey, Frank explored the vast landscape of practical applications and innovations in the field of electricity. From household appliances to renewable energy systems, from communication networks to medical devices, electricity played a pivotal role in shaping the world. Frank marveled at the ingenuity and creativity of inventors and engineers who harnessed the power of electricity to improve lives and drive progress. One inventor caught the attention of Frank, her name was Lilly. Lilly worked at a chocolate factory and was responsible for new machinery automation, and she also designed electrical circuits to help production run more efficiently.

Chapter 8: The Power of Knowledge and Imagination through automation

As Frank concluded his journey into the realm of electricity, he realized that true power lay not just in understanding the principles of circuits and currents but also in harnessing the boundless potential of knowledge and imagination. Frank learned about machine automation using PLC's and found that there is quite a calling for seasoned PLC programmers. He was so impressed by the adventure of learning about electricity and automation that he contacted his local electrical union and signed on as an apprentice. He was assigned a job at a local chocolate manufacturing plant where he met Lilly, a PLC programmer, electrical engineer and inventor. Lilly and Frank worked together on a few automation projects and Frank learned about ladder logic and how a PLC can control automation as well as process control. One day there was a power surge at the plant which sent too much voltage to the PLC power supply. The chocolate factory production stopped all at once.

Frank worked with another electrician, Mark, to find the source of the power surge, The source of the power surge was caused by a malfunctioning transformer at the power plant. Frank and Mark, the Journeyman electrician suggested a surge protector for the PLC to keep it isolated from power surges. They installed the surge protector and after they powered up the plant he noticed the teamwork of Lilly, and the other engineers as they worked to get the plant back up and running. Lilly found several pieces of the ladder logic that needed to be re-written. Once they got the plant back up and running, the chocolates were even better than before thanks to Lilly's new code for batch control, and process control. Lilly explained to Frank how a PLC could help make a process more efficient because a PLC was a computer. With a PLC most human errors can be eliminated, and a company's product quality will improve. There is always a need for skilled programmers, electricians, Plumbers, and carpenters.

Frank continued his education and became one of the top design engineers at the chocolate factory. Lilly got a degree in electrical engineering and continued to work at the chocolate factory.

Epilogue:

And so, Frank and Lilly's epic voyage into the world of electricity ends, but their thirst for knowledge and exploration knew no bounds. As they looked out at the horizon, filled with the promise of new discoveries and challenges, they knew that the journey was far from over. Armed with the wisdom gained from their adventures, Frank and Lilly stood ready to embrace the mysteries of the universe and illuminate the path for others to follow.

This is the first in a series of automation books.

CHAPTER 9: SHORT STORIES

The following short stories are mostly fiction, but the message is clear, A good education in a trade school is necessary for anyone interested in pursuing a career in auto mechanics, industrial manufacturing mechanics, industrial electricity, and industrial automation. I personally chose industrial electricity and automation along with industrial electronics. This career path has allowed me to almost write my own ticket for work. I get calls every day asking me if I would be interested in working for different manufacturing companies. I have attended classes at Rockwell Automation for Allen Bradley PLC's and motion control. I have worked with some of the top automation engineers in the industry and they have taught me everything I know today about machine automation and controls.

1) "LILLY'S QUEST FOR ELECTRICAL KNOWLEGE"

Once upon a time in a small village nestled at the foot of a majestic mountain, there lived a curious young inventor named Lilly. Lilly was known everywhere for her insatiable thirst for knowledge and her unrelenting passion for tinkering with gadgets and gizmos. Lilly attended a trade school that offered electrical engineering classes.

One day, as Lilly was exploring the depths of the village's library, she stumbled upon an ancient tome filled with illustrations of strange contraptions powered by a mysterious force called electricity. Intrigued by these fantastical designs, Lilly became determined to unlock the secrets of this enigmatic energy source. While in the library she met a young engineer named Frank. Frank was also on a quest to learn as much about electricity as possible. Lilly and Frank started talking about the possibilities of harnessing the power of electricity to run industrial machinery. They compared notes and Lilly was impressed by Franks knowledge of electricity and engineering. She suggested that he enroll in the same engineering classes that she was taking.

Armed with nothing but her wits and a fervent desire to learn, plus help from Frank, Lilly set out to create her own electrical device. She scoured the village for spare parts, scavenging broken toys and discarded tools to cobble together a crude apparatus that she hoped would harness the power of electricity and power the city's streetlights. Frank provided lots of books and notes that he took over the past year to help Lilly figure out the math for current draw, maximum voltages for her invention and how to automate the machine using a series of contactors, and a PLC.

After many long days and sleepless nights of trial and error, Lilly finally succeeded in creating a small device that crackled with energy. With trembling hands, she flipped a switch, and to her amazement, a tiny bulb at the end of the contraption glowed with a warm, gentle light. The machine had several A/C contactors and a terminal strip to land the wires on. The light that she saw was the power light and Lilly and Frank wired the contactors to the street light power grid. Lilly pressed the first switch and a bunch of 10 streetlights came to life.

Overwhelmed with joy and wonder, Lilly shared her invention with the villagers, who were awestruck by the magical glow emanating from the device, and how easily she could control the streetlights. They marveled at the possibilities of this newfound power and the potential for innovation and progress it held. They wondered how many other machines automated and other companies were taking notice of Lilly's inventions. As word of Lilly's invention spread everywhere, travelers from distant lands flocked to the village to witness the marvel of electricity. Scientists, engineers, and inventors came together to collaborate with Lilly, each bringing their unique expertise to further harness the power of this revolutionary force. Together, they built grand machines that illuminated the darkness, powered mills, and factories, and transformed the way people lived and worked. The village blossomed into a bustling hub of innovation and progress, all thanks to the spark of creativity that Lily had ignited with her invention. And so, the legacy of Lilly and her discovery of electricity lived on, inspiring generations to push the boundaries of what was possible and to dream of a future powered by innovation and imagination. Lilly signed on with a chocolate factory and was responsible for all of the automation, and new machine design.

2) "The Electric Revolution"

In the bustling industrial city of Vol Tania, where factories hummed with activity and smokestacks towered over the skyline, there lived a young engineer named Mia. Mia was fascinated by the power of electricity and its potential to revolutionize the way industries operated. She dreamed of harnessing this power to drive innovation and efficiency in the factories that fueled the city's economy.

One day, a massive blackout struck Vol Tania, causing chaos and disruption in the industrial sector. Machines ground to a halt, production lines stalled, and workers were left in the dark. Mia saw this as a wake-up call, a sign that the city's reliance on outdated power systems was holding back progress and putting the economy at risk.

Determined to bring about change, Mia set out to electrify the factories of Vol Tania. She designed a comprehensive plan to upgrade the power infrastructure, replacing outdated steam engines with electric motors and implementing a network of generators and transformers to ensure a stable and reliable power supply. The city's industrial leaders were initially skeptical of Mia's ambitious proposal, but she persevered, driven by a vision of a more efficient and sustainable future for Vol Tania.

As the industrial sector gradually transitioned to electric power, the transformation in Voltania was nothing short of revolutionary. Factories that once relied on cumbersome steam engines now hummed with the quiet efficiency of electric motors, boosting productivity and reducing operating costs. Workers found themselves in a safer and more comfortable environment, free from the noise and smoke of the past.

The electrification of Vol Tania's industries also brought about unexpected benefits. With the adoption of electric power, the city's factories became more environmentally friendly, reducing pollution and mitigating the impact on the surrounding ecosystem. Vol Tania gained a reputation as a forward-thinking city that prioritized sustainability and innovation, attracting investments and skilled workers from everywhere.

As the years passed, Vol Tania flourished as a beacon of industrial progress, thanks to Mia's vision and determination to harness the power of electricity for the greater good. His efforts not only modernized the city's factories but also inspired a new generation of engineers and inventors to explore the endless possibilities of industrial electricity.

And as Marcus stood atop a hill overlooking the vibrant city of Vol Tania, with its gleaming factories and humming power lines stretching into the horizon, he knew that the electric revolution he had sparked would continue to illuminate the path towards a brighter, more efficient future for generations to come.

3) "The Rise of Automation"

In a bustling city named Tech Topia, where technology and innovation were at the heart of everything, there lived a young engineer named Tammy. Tammy was fascinated by machines and automation from an early age. She spent countless hours tinkering with robots and programming intricate systems that could perform tasks with precision and efficiency.

One day, a renowned tech company in Tech Topia called Automatics announced the launch of their latest invention - a revolutionary automated workforce. These machines were designed to perform a wide range of tasks, from manufacturing to customer service, with minimal human intervention. The city was abuzz with excitement and curiosity about these new machines that promised to revolutionize the way people worked.

As the automated workforce was gradually introduced into various industries, Tammy found herself at a crossroads. On the one hand, she was amazed by the capabilities of these machines and the potential they held to streamline processes and boost productivity. On the other hand, she couldn't shake off the nagging feeling that the widespread adoption of automation could lead to job losses and economic upheaval for many in the city.

Determined to understand the implications of automation, Tammy delved deep into research and conversations with experts in the field. She learned about the benefits of automation, such as increased efficiency, reduced errors, and improved safety in hazardous environments. However, she also discovered the challenges, including job displacement, the need for retraining, and the widening gap between the skilled and unskilled workforce.

As time passed, the impact of automation became more apparent in Techtopia. While some industries flourished and saw unprecedented growth with the help of machines, others struggled to adapt to the changing landscape. Unemployment rates rose, and social unrest simmered as people grappled with the uncertainty of their future in a world increasingly dominated by automation.

Feeling a sense of responsibility to her community, Tammy decided to act. She founded a tech academy that offered training programs to help people develop the skills needed to thrive in the age of automation. She also collaborated with local businesses to create job opportunities that complemented the work of machines, rather than replacing them.

Through her efforts, Tammy bridged the gap between humans and machines, fostering a symbiotic relationship where automation enhanced human capabilities rather than overshadowing them. Together, they ushered in a new era of innovation and progress in Tech Topia, where people and technology worked hand in hand to build a brighter future for all.

In the end, Tammy realized that the true power of automation lay not in replacing humans, but in empowering them to reach new heights of creativity and productivity. And as she looked out at the cityscape of Tech Topia, bustling with activity and innovation, she knew that the future held endless possibilities for those who embraced the transformative potential of machines and automation.

4) "Sparks of Innovation"

In the small town of Sparks Ville, nestled amidst rolling hills and lush greenery, there lived a brilliant inventor named Emily. Emily was fascinated by electricity and automation since she was a child, spending hours experimenting with circuits and building automated devices in her workshop. One day, a massive thunderstorm swept through Sparksville, knocking out the power grid and plunging the town into darkness. Emily saw this as an opportunity to showcase the potential of electricity and automation to transform their lives. Determined to bring light and innovation to her community, she set out to create something truly groundbreaking. Using her knowledge and skills, Emily designed a system of automated streetlights powered by renewable energy sources. She installed solar panels on the rooftops of buildings and connected them to a network of battery storage units. These batteries would store excess energy generated during the day and power the streetlights at night, ensuring that the town remained brightly lit even during power outages.

As word spread about Emily's invention, the townspeople marveled at her ingenuity and foresight. They embraced automated streetlights not just for their functionality but also for their environmental sustainability. Sparks Ville became a beacon of innovation, attracting visitors from everywhere who were eager to witness the marriage of electricity and automation in action. Inspired by the success of her streetlight project, Emily embarked on a new endeavor to automate the town's water supply system. She developed sensors that could monitor water levels in reservoirs and control the flow of water through pipelines with precision and efficiency. This automation not only optimized water usage but also ensured a reliable supply for the townspeople, even during droughts or emergencies. She installed a series of radio telemetry to send water tower signals to a central PLC located in the main utility building. There the engineers and maintenance staff can operate any of the city's water towers.

As Emily's inventions continued to improve the quality of life in Sparks Ville, she caught the attention of a prominent tech company looking to invest in innovative technologies. They offered her a partnership to scale up her projects and bring her innovations to a global audience. With their support, Emily's dream of leveraging electricity and automation to create a more sustainable and connected world became a reality. Years passed, and Sparks Ville transformed into a hub of technological advancement, with Emily at the forefront of groundbreaking innovations in energy and automation. Her legacy inspired a new generation of inventors and engineers to push the boundaries of what was possible, harnessing the power of electricity and automation to shape a brighter future for all, and as the sun set over Sparks Ville, casting a warm glow on the automated streetlights that illuminated the town, Emily knew that her journey was far from over. With a spark of creativity and a heart full of passion, she continued to pioneer new ways to harness the power of electricity and automation for the betterment of society, one invention at a time.

5) "ALEX AND THE TRADE SCHOOL"

Once upon a time, in a bustling town nestled between the mountains, there was a trade school known as Valley Forge Trade School. This school was a beacon of opportunity for young individuals who sought to learn practical skills and crafts that would set them on a path to a fulfilling career.

Among the students at Valley Forge Trade School was a young man named Alex. Unlike many of his peers who chose traditional academic paths, Alex had always been drawn to working with his hands. He had a natural talent for fixing things and a passion for creating with tools and machinery.

At Valley Forge Trade School, Alex found his calling in the field of automotive mechanics. Under the guidance of skilled instructors, he learned how to diagnose engine problems, repair brakes, and perform routine maintenance on a variety of vehicles. He spent hours in the school's garage, covered in grease and sweat, but with a smile on his face as he honed his craft.

As the months passed, Alex's skills grew rapidly. He participated in local competitions and won awards for his exceptional workmanship. His dedication and passion for his trade did not go unnoticed, and soon he caught the eye of a local auto repair shop owner, Mr. Jenkins.

Impressed by Alex's talent and work ethic, Mr. Jenkins offered him an apprenticeship at his shop. Overjoyed at the opportunity to turn his passion into a career, Alex accepted without hesitation. He continued to attend classes at Valley Forge Trade School during the day and worked at the shop in the evenings and on weekends.

With each passing day, Alex gained more experience and confidence in his abilities. He learned the ins and outs of running a successful auto repair business, from customer service to inventory management. His hard work paid off, and soon he was entrusted with more complex repair jobs and responsibilities.

Years went by, and Alex became a respected and sought-after mechanic in the town. His reputation for quality work and honesty spread everywhere, bringing in customers from neighboring towns and cities. He never forgot his roots at Valley Forge Trade School, where he had laid the foundation for his successful career.

One day, as Alex stood in the garage of his own auto repair shop, surrounded by tools and the hum of engines, he couldn't help but feel a deep sense of gratitude for the trade school that had shaped his destiny. He knew that without the skills and knowledge he had gained at Valley Forge Trade School, he would not be where he was today.

And so, Alex continued to work with passion and dedication, passing on his knowledge and expertise to the next generation of aspiring mechanics who walked through the doors of Valley Forge Trade School, just as he had done so many years ago. In this way, the legacy of the trade school lived on, empowering individuals like Alex to pursue their dreams and build a brighter future through the power of hands-on learning and practical skills.

6) "SARA AND THE MECHANICS"

Once upon a time in a small town nestled in the rolling hills, there was a bustling manufacturing plant that produced intricate machinery used in various industries. The heartbeat of this plant was its team of dedicated maintenance mechanic who worked tirelessly to ensure that the machines ran smoothly and efficiently. Among the team was a young mechanic named Sarah, known for her keen eye for detail and unwavering dedication to her craft. Sarah had always been fascinated by how things worked and took considerable pride in her role as a maintenance mechanic, and she graduated at the top of her class at Valley Forge Trade school for industrial maintenance mechanics.

One day, a crucial machine in the plant broke down unexpectedly, causing a halt in production and sending the workers into a frenzy. Sarah was called upon to investigate and fix the issue, knowing that the entire plant's operations depended on her skills. With her trusty toolkit in hand, Sarah dove headfirst into troubleshooting the machine, carefully inspecting each component and running diagnostic tests to pinpoint the problem. Hours passed as she meticulously worked to identify the root cause of the breakdown. As the sun began to set and the plant fell quiet, Sarah finally discovered the faulty part that had caused the machine to malfunction. Without hesitation, she set to work repairing and replacing the component, her hands moving deftly as she brought the machine back to life. When the first rays of dawn peeked over the horizon, the machine hummed back to life, its gears turning smoothly once more. The plant sprang back to action, and the workers cheered as production resumed. Sarah's fellow mechanics praised her for her quick thinking and technical prowess, acknowledging her as a true master of her craft. From that day on, Sarah became known as the go-to mechanic for any maintenance challenge in the plant, earning the respect and admiration of her colleagues. As the days turned into weeks and the weeks into months, Sarah continued to excel in her role, ensuring that the machinery in the plant ran like clockwork. Her passion for maintenance mechanics shone brightly, inspiring others to strive for excellence in their work. And so, the small town's manufacturing plant thrived, thanks to the dedication and skill of Sarah and her team of maintenance technicians who kept the wheels of industry turning smoothly.

7) **Title: The Symphony of Process Control**

In the heart of an industrial city, where machines hummed in harmony and flames danced in the furnaces, there stood a grand factory known as Creston Industries. Within its walls, a symphony of process control played out every day, orchestrated by a team of skilled engineers led by the brilliant mind of Dr. Alexander Reed.

Dr. Reed was a man of precision and vision, known throughout the industry for his mastery of process control. With his guidance, Creston Industries had become a beacon of efficiency and innovation, producing goods of unparalleled quality and consistency.

One day, a new challenge presented itself to Dr. Reed and his team. A crucial component of the manufacturing process had begun to show signs of instability, threatening to disrupt the delicate balance that kept the factory running smoothly. As alarms blared and workers rushed to contain the problem, Dr. Reed calmly assessed the situation and called for a meeting of his team.

Gathered in the control room, surrounded by monitors displaying intricate graphs and charts, Dr. Reed outlined the issue at hand. With a sense of urgency but also confidence, he assigned tasks to each team member, drawing upon their individual strengths and expertise.

Together, they dove into the problem, analyzing data, running simulations, and testing hypotheses with meticulous care.

Hours turned into days as the team worked tirelessly, each member playing their part in the intricate dance of process control. Through collaboration and unwavering dedication, they identified the root cause of the issue and devised a solution that would not only restore stability to the manufacturing process but also enhance it beyond its previous capabilities.

As the factory returned to its usual rhythm, Dr. Reed stood before his team, a sense of pride and gratitude shining in his eyes. He praised their efforts, acknowledging the crucial role that each person had played in overcoming the challenge they had faced. Together, they had proven the power of teamwork, expertise, and determination in the realm of process control.

From that day on, Creston Industries stood as a shining example of excellence in process control, a testament to the vision and leadership of Dr. Alexander Reed and the unwavering dedication of his team. The symphony of process control continued to play out within its walls, a harmonious blend of precision, innovation, and teamwork that echoed through the industrial city and beyond.

And so, the story of Creston Industries became legend, inspiring future generations of engineers and technicians to strive for greatness in the art of process control, knowing that with the right combination of skill, collaboration, and determination, anything was possible.

More about Frank and Lilly:

In the town of Jacksonville Florida, lived a young engineer named Frank. He had always been captivated by the magic of automation. Frank was a meticulous design engineer and was well known at the Jacksonville chocolate factory for his innovative designs and his attention to detail. Lilly, a seasoned plc programmer and automation engineer had a passion for all things automated, and their paths were destined to intertwine.

Franks story:

Frank Hanson had started his career as an electrician working in manufacturing. His friend and mentor Mark Gracey, a master electrician at the Jacksonville Chocolate factory, had signed off on all of Frank's hours so he could take the test to get his Journeyman Electrician License. Frank worked as an electrician at the Chocolate factory and got his master electrician license after a year of working for his friend. Frank loved being an electrician but thought he would be better suited for machine design. Frank continued to work as an electrician at the chocolate factory while attending a local college for mechanical engineering. He graduated at the top of his class with honors and was hired by the Chocolate Factory as a design engineer.

Frank started designing machinery at the Chocolate Factory that would revolutionize the candy bar industry. One of his designs was a packaging machine that would package 200 candy bars in a carton, send the carton through a printer and onto a conveyor belt that would send the carton to a staging area to be palletized. The design worked, but the cartons were loaded onto a pallet by hand and then manually sent to a wrapping machine. The process was quite slow, and the company wanted to increase production. Frank had heard about automation and even read a few books on how to automate manufacturing machinery. What the company lacked was an automation engineer who could take his designs to the next level and increase production of candy bars.

Frank Hanson sat at his desk at the Jacksonville Chocolate factory pondering his next project. He was wondering how he could improve on the conveyor delivery system in packaging. He was looking over his design when his computer chimed with an email inviting him to the upcoming Inovatech annual tech fair in Tampa Florida. The fair venue included speakers from all over describing their latest designs and inventions, plus several classes on automation and controls. Frank decided to attend the automation fair and signed up for all the seminars.

On the day of the tech fair, Frank attended a one-hour lecture about automating a conveyor belt in a manufacturing plant, led by Lilly Hart, an automation engineer with 15 years' experience designing control schemes for all kinds of designs. Lilly was attractive blonde, and Frank was quite taken by her knowledge of automation and the sound of her voice. Frank took many notes and was impressed by one of her designs. It was a groundbreaking smart conveyor that was attached to a packing machine.

After the lecture was over Frank stayed after everyone left the room and asked Lilly if she would have time to have coffee with him to discuss his latest design. She agreed to meet him in an hour at the food court.

Lilly's story:

Lilly had always been fascinated by how things electrical worked. As a child, she would take apart old radios, examining their intricate parts and putting them back together. This curiosity blossomed into a passion for technology as she grew older. All through high school, she knew she wanted to pursue a career in technology, but it wasn't until she heard about a workshop on Programmable Logic Controllers (PLCs) that her high school was hosting.

The workshop was hosted at a local community college, and Lilly loved the hands-on approach of the instructor. She watched as he described in detail how PLCs were used to automate machinery in factories.

When she graduated high school, she enrolled in a technical program at the local community college where the workshop was held. The program she enrolled in focused on PLC programming. The first few weeks were quite challenging. The terminology felt foreign, but Lilly was determined to learn everything about programing a PLC. She spent late nights in the lab, experimenting with code and troubleshooting her projects. With each small success—a blinking light here, a motor that spun correctly there—her confidence grew.

One day, as her programing got more complicated, she faced a problem that had stumped her for hours. She was programming a PLC to control a conveyor belt system, but her code just was not executing as expected. Frustrated, she stepped outside for a breath of fresh air. As she sat on a bench, her mind raced with possibilities. Suddenly, an idea struck her: what if she simplified the logic?

When she returned to the lab, she rewrote the program, breaking it down into smaller, more manageable parts. This time, when she downloaded the code, the conveyor belt whirred to life, moving smoothly along its path. Lilly's face lit up with joy.

As the weeks turned into months, Lilly's skills sharpened. She began to work on more complex projects, including a fully automated assembly line simulation. Her instructors took notice of her dedication and creativity, often asking her to help her classmates who were struggling. Lilly found joy in teaching others what she had learned.

One afternoon, her instructor approached her with an exciting opportunity at Inovatech a local manufacturing company. They were looking for an intern to help with a major automation project. Lilly thought It was exactly the kind of practical experience she had been hoping for.

With her instructor's recommendation, Lilly got the internship. On her first day, she was introduced to the team, a mix of seasoned engineers and fresh-faced interns. Lilly felt both nervous and excited. The project was bigger than she had first imagined. They needed to upgrade an outdated assembly line with an ultramodern PLC system.

As the weeks progressed, Lilly immersed herself in the project and breaking down the code into smaller bites that were more manageable. She spent hours collaborating with her team, learning the existing system. She found many bugs in the code, hardware incompatibilities and a network that also needed upgrading. With each problem solved, she felt more like a part of the team.

On the day of the system launch, Lilly stood nervously beside her colleagues, watching as they prepared to test the new automation system.

Lilly held her breath as the team started the program. The machines sprang to life, and the assembly line began to work seamlessly. A wave of relief and pride washed over her; all their hard work had paid off.

As the team celebrated their success, Lilly reflected on her journey. From a curious girl taking apart toys to a confident PLC programmer, she had come a long way. She knew this was just the beginning, and she was surprised when the owner of Inovatech offered her a position in the automation department.

Lilly was excited and nervous about working in a manufacturing environment. For one thing money was tight, and her projects were often put on hold. When there was not much to do, she continued to hone her skills as a PLC programmer and automation engineer. She went to automation fairs around the country selling Inovatech state of the art automatic conveyors and demonstrating how an automated conveyor coupled with a palletizer and barcodes could help organize any food manufacturer that warehouses pallets of cases of product. From soda pop to pasta Lilly was the go-to engineer. She can solve any automation problem or design flaw.

She had a career that was built on hard work, dedication to her trade, but she was very lonely and wanted something more from her life, and that something could be Frank.

Frank meets with Lilly at the coffee shop:

Frank got a table at the coffee shop and just sat down when Lilly came in. She sat down and asked him what she could do for him. Frank went into detail about his new conveyor project. He described how he can design an ultramodern mechanical conveyor, but he went on to say that he lacked the automation experience to brink the project to life. Frank told Lilly that the Chocolate Factory did not have an automation engineering department, but they needed one. Lilly asked if Frank had a vision for what that department would look like. What projects were available after the conveyor project was completed. She also asked about how long to complete the current project.

Frank said he was under quite a bit of pressure to complete the project. He said he has the design completed and the approval for the money. As Frank talked with passion about the project at hand, Lilly was quite impressed with how thorough Frank was at his job. Something that she also prided herself on.

Lilly said, "so Frank, are you able to create an automation engineering department? Frank said yes, but he does not have allot of time to spend creating a job description and advertise and interview for the position. Lilly thought about it for a while and said, we can work out a deal with me under contract to help with the project. If your happy with my work I would be interested in starting your automation engineering department as a direct hire. Frank thought about that suggestion for only a minute and, said he would like to pursue her offer. "Would you have time today to come to the Jacksonville Chocolate Factory? Lilly said she could be there first thing tomorrow morning." They shook hands to seal the deal, and they parted ways.

THE CHOCOLATE FACTORY:

Lilly drove to Jacksonville that afternoon and checked into the hotel that was close to the factory. She got a good night sleep, and, in the morning, she met Frank in the lobby of the chocolate factory. "Good morning, Lilly, I hope you had a nice night. Yes, it was very restful thank you for asking. Frank walked with Lilly to H.R. and introduced her to Heather, they H.R. supervisor. He explained what Lilly's role in the project was. After an hour of signing confidential forms, going over the wages, and after an hour Lilly was more than ready to get started. Frank went to H.R. and brought Lilly to her office and introduced her to his team.

Lilly was impressed with Franks team, and they brought out their AutoCAD drawings and described their vision for the conveyor. Lilly asked about the budget she would have to work with, and Frank said whatever she needed. In fact, the more Frank and his team talked about the project the more excited she was getting. After 2 hours of talking and going over machine schematics and expectations, Lilly had already formed a control scheme in her head. She asked about sensors and instrumentation. Frank said she would oversee ordering all electronics, motors, motor controllers and programming.

Lilly could not believe she could get into a position on the ground floor. She was excited not only for the project, but also to be able to build a world class automation department. I also helped that she was interested in Frank outside of the office, but she was shy and unsure of how to process these feelings. After a long day of going over the project, she was ready to have a quiet evening at the hotel. When she arrived at her room, there was a bouquet of flowers on the desk. They were from Frank thanking her for helping him and his team. Lilly felt a flutter in the pit of her stomach, something she had never felt before. Lilly texted the owner of Inova Tech and asked if he would meet with her over zoom in an hour. He agreed and, in the hour, she wrote a very in-depth resignation letter to the owner.

When they got online with the video call she was surprised to see the owner, her immediate supervisor, and the head of HR. After some unpleasant greetings and small talk, the owner of Inova Tech spoke first. "How's it going up there in Jacksonville Lilly? She explained that she was doing a bit of consulting for the Jacksonville Chocolate Factory. All three of the managers wanted to know exactly what her role was in consulting. Lilly was getting a bit uneasy with the dialog and asked, "why do you ask all these questions?" They all exchanged glances, and the owner cleared his throat and said "we are cutting our budget for next year and we need to eliminate your position. The money for new projects has dried up a bit and we are faced with just running with the current machinery." Lilly almost leaped out of her chair because she was so happy to hear the news. The owner went on to tell her that she would be getting a nice severance package which is why HR was in on the meeting. The HR director started talking about her severance package. "Lilly, because of your position in the company and your dedication to helping the company succeed this far, the board of directors has unanimously agreed to award you 3 years of severance along with full medical benefits for the 3 years. We are deeply sorry that we have put you in this position and want you to take as much time as you need to find a new company to call your home. You will be missed.

"Your termination will be effective immediately and I will e-mail you the forms you need to sign. We already have your bank information so a direct deposit will be made at the end of this week. Do you have any questions?" Lilly thought for a few minutes and said "no, I understand everything, and I am grateful for the years I have spent at Inova Tech. They end the meeting, and Lilly is overwhelmed with joy at the prospect of starting a new career at the Chocolate Factory, even though she is only under contract.

The next day Lilly is at her desk early, before anyone is in the front office. Sha can hear the machinery working in the factory and decides to take a walk and see the operation. As she walks around the factory the smells are very enticing, she watches how the chocolate is poured into molds for candy bars, and how the caramel is injected into chocolate balls, and other machinery that combines it with peanuts. she starts to wonder about batch control and process control.

As she watched each mold being filled with different chocolates, she noticed some inconsistencies in the chocolate look and how sometimes the chocolate would flow easy and sometimes it seemed to be a bit thicker. Lilly went to her office to look up the recipes for the different batches and by then Frank was there. Lilly asked him if she could take a look at the controls for the current batch control because of what she found. "Frank, I found some inconsistencies in the batch control that really could use some attention." Frank said "We had a company come in and do a software update last week and since then it seems the chocolate has not been the same quality we are used to. If you can fix the problem, we would be very grateful."

Lilly got her laptop and a table and chair and went out to the factory production floor. She set up by the mixing vats and holding tanks and logged onto the PLC. As she looked at the data, she noticed that the temperatures were fluctuating quite allot. She looked at the calibration of each sensor and there was no log entry of when they were last calibrated. As she looked further into the data, she noticed that the software update was never tested. Lilly went to the production supervisor Hanna, and introduced herself. She explained to Hanna what she found and asked if she could do some improvements to the code and change the current batch control so they wouldn't have any more quality issues. Hanna was very excited to have the problems solved with the current system and gave Lilly the okay to fix and upgrade the current system.

Lilly rolled up her sleeves and got to work rewriting the code, and testing the software upgrade on a simulating program she has installed on her laptop.

The simulation showed a bug in the new software that would prevent any automatic calibration checks and she quickly rewrote some code in the software operating system to fix that problem. After that was completed and tested several times, she rewrote the batch control scheme for all the different chocolate recipes. Once that was completed, she loaded the new code into the simulator and watched as everything started working flawlessly. After she was satisfied with the end result, she went to talk with Hanna again. "Hanna, I have completed all the necessary changes to the batch control and the new software that was installed last week. With your permission I want to download the new software and the new batch control. Thats great Lilly, go ahead and load what you need". Lilly and Hanna go the batch control room and Hanna watches as Lilly loads the new software, and once that is completed Lilly downloads the new batch control. When that is completed, she switches the processor back to run, and they watch as the temperatures are rock steady and the level controls and the timing of the batch are in sync.

As the first batch of chocolate is dispensed into the molds the smell is mouthwatering and everyone is amazed at how the consistency of the chocolate is creamier and flows perfect into the molds. Hanna is very impressed and she and Lilly go to the monitors that control the entire system. The monitor shows chocolate quality and after they have run for an hour Hanna shows Lilly the before and after quality of the chocolate. Before the changes the quality was at 60 percent and they were trying to figure out why. After Lillys new program was installed the quality over the past hour was at 100 percent, and with the new software upgrade Lilly repaired the output was at 98 percent. Hanna explained that they have never achieved that kind of numbers.

Lilly was very happy and in her head was thinking how grateful she was to have a good education and knowledge of how manufacturing machinery works.

Lilly worked tirelessly on the new conveyor machinery and as Franks team of mechanical engineers brought in the machinery, the Maintenance techs got involved in the installation of the new equipment. There were 2 new maintenance tech named Matt and John. They were only with the company for 4 months but already have made an impression on everyone at the chocolate factory. Their work ethic and innovative approach to problems and new designs was impressive. Lilly asked for Matt and John to work on her team (she was still the only automation engineer) and she filled them in on how the machinery worked. The tree of them worked long hours installing the machinery and running miles of conduit for all the sensors Lilly had purchased. She and John and Matt pulled all the wire to the new PLC cabinet and Lilly had John wire everything in the cabinet while Matt finished the mechanical alignment of the conveyor, and installed the new bar code printers.

After working long hours for 3 months installing the machinery and programming the new automation into the current packing machinery, they were finally ready to start the equipment. Lilly had run simulations of the program for a week and had re wrote some of the code so now it was working perfect on the simulations.

As Frank and Lilly along with John and Matt were at the control panel to test the machinery for the first time the owner of the Jacksonville Chocolate Factory came out to observe the startup. Lilly pressed the start button on the screen and the machinery came to life. On the screen the graphics showed conveyor speed, the status of the bar code printers, the current palletizer pattern, how full the conveyor for dispensing to the palletizer, and how many cases have been produced. Lilly went to have the operators start the packers and when the first carton went through the bar code printer and up the conveyor and stopped at the front of the first conveyor before the palletizer, a cheer went up in the factory.

They all watched in awe as the cartons filled the first conveyor, and when the last carton passed the full sensor, the conveyor started smoothly and the cartons advanced to the palletizer and when there were 6 layers the pallet lowered and was ejected to the shrink wrapper. When that was completed, the pallet moved out and had a bar code pressed onto it and the stopped and waited to be transported to the warehouse.

Frank was the first to speak "Lilly, you have helped us achieve a successful project completion, without your expert knowledge and dedication we would not have succeeded so quickly. The owner of the Jacksonville Chocolate Factory was also impressed and requested that Lilly come to his office at the end of her day. Lilly turned to John and Matt and said "thanks to your dedication to your trades we have successfully completed the first of many projects. It was truly a pleasure working on this project with you both.

At the end of her shift feeling quite exhausted, Lilly made her way to the owner's office and knocked on his door. "Come in miss Hagen" said the owner, his name was Joseph. Joseph was a portly man with a face that reminded Lilly of her grandfather. As she entered Joseph's office, he picked up the phone and made a quick call. Lilly sat down and Joseph started the conversation "Miss Hagen, your work since you started 6 months ago has been top notch.

Hanna has told me that the chocolate has never looked or tasted better after you upgraded the batch controls and the software. Now with Franks project you have demonstrated that your abilities are versatile in every aspect of manufacturing.

There was a knock-on Josephs door and Heather from HR and Frank came in. Joseph said that Frank had something to say. "Lilly, we have enjoyed having you work under contract over the past 6 months. The chocolate has never tasted to good, and you have improved the batch controls so Hanna can now keep track of which recipe is working and how quality has improved.

The new conveyor project was completed 2 months early thanks to your dedication and knowledge of automation. We would like to offer you a permanent position here at the chocolate factory. Your salary will be $210,000.00 to start along with a quarterly bonus of 10 percent of your wages. If you would like to think about our offer that's quite understandable." Lilly thought for a couple minutes and finally said "I would be honored to work here at the chocolate factory and call this my home. I accept your offer. Thats great Lilly said Frank, and Heather asked Lilly to stop by her office first thing in the morning to go over her new position. Before the meeting adjourned, Lilly asked if she could put together an automation department. Everyone agreed that it would be in the best interest of the company to have a formal automation department that could handle day to day troubleshooting and machine upgrades.

Lilly asked if she could bring John and Matt into the automation department as her apprentices, at a wage of $110,000.00 each. Joseph agreed to her request and Heather said she would take care of the offers in the morning.

Lilly and Frank started dating shortly after Lilly was offered her position and they were married one year later. John and Matt continued to work for Lilly and John went to many Rockwell Engineering classes and got a degree in PLC programming. John and Lilly work together on many automation projects and with the help of Matts fabrication skills have built a department that has brought the Jacksonville Chocolate Factory recognition as the leader in the candy bar industry.

Notes from the author:

This book has been fun to write and share my experiences in manufacturing automation and controls. I have been learning PLC code since 1988 and I have had many successes and lots of failures. When Lilly re-wrote the batch control and it worked flawlessly the first time, she started it is almost unheard of, even with a good simulation.

I started my career as an auto mechanic and decided early on that I wanted something better. A friend got me a job at a manufacturing plant in the

maintenance department working on manufacturing machinery.

I loved working on manufacturing machinery and I had a wonderful mentor. Then one day we had to remove some lab equipment and my supervisor said he turned off the power. I reached as far a I could to cut the wires and was immediately hooked into a live wire with my nose firmly grounded on a conduit. My teeth were clacking together at 60hz and my muscles gripped the side cutters tighter. I'm still not sure how I managed to fling the side cutters, but I did and fell from the shelf I was standing on. I was holding my nose when my co-workers came running to see what happened. When I pointed to the open box, they both started laughing because my nose had second degree burns and was blistered. I talked with my supervisor about what happened and he just said he must have shut the wrong breaker off. In this business there is no room for error and knowledge is everything. I asked if I could take some classes at the local vo-tech college and was surprised that my supervisor said the company would pay as long as I got a passing grade. I signed up for night classes in basic electricity the next day.

It took me a long time to recover emotionally from that nose burn, I remember needing to climb a 12-foot ladder to unhook some wires for a machine we were going to move. I was told again the power was turned off, but I was very skeptical. I walked around that ladder for a good 10 minutes before one of my co-workers noticed me and asked if I wanted him to take care of it. I quickly nodded yes and we kept it just between us. But I quickly gained confidence and once I got my own digital volt meter, I could check my own voltages (something everyone should learn if you are going to work with electricity) My classes were going great and I started to enroll in more and more classes about electricity. I wanted to get a journeyman electrician license in the worst way. But the company I worked for did not have a master electrician on record so I was out of luck for getting any hours signed off. (You need 8000 hours working under a master in a credited apprenticeship program) I was determined to succeed and kept going to technical college, then one day the company got into some automation using an Allen Bradley PLC.

I asked if I could attend some classes on how to program the new PLC but was shot down because I wasn't an engineer. I kept on learning and the company bought books on programing an Allen Bradley PLC. The first generations were dos based and, and then they went to a windows environment with the new RSLogix 500 software. I learned how to use the software but not how to download to a processor. As the company grew into automation, I was asked to take on a small project that used a processor called a SLC500. The project was for a test bench that was being designed by the engineering department. I worked with an engineer on the programing and when we downloaded the project it was full of code that did not work correctly. I have always said if you want to know how to fix a computer, break if unintentionally and then try to fix it. This is exactly what happened with my first program. And Allen Bradley had a thing called online programming. (This was before any simulations was available) I was able to go online and fix my code one rung at a time. (A PLC uses ladder logic)

Once I learned how to program online without taking down the machinery things got better for me. I kept going to Rockwell Engineering classes for motion control, programing from scratch, PLC troubleshooting, GML programing (graphical machine language), servo motors, networking, and C++ programming. Along with getting an associate's degree in electronics I was on my way. I became an expert troubleshooter with electrical circuits and electronics.

Being an expert also means you are in demand and sometimes you can be a bit too tired. One night I got called in because an operator zip tied some wires on a drop for some servo motors. When they pressed the start button and the machine sent the robotic gantry in motion all the wires were pulled out of the ceiling, and the machine was dead in the water. I was so tired from work and school that I made an error. I got all the wires hooked back up, then got my laptop out and logged into the motion computer, the one that programmed in C++.

I wasn't paying attention and must have pressed the delete program button, or I fat fingered it. Either way, as I looked at my screen with the live data from the memory, it was blank. No matter what I did to recover the program was of no use, it was gone. I phone the engineer who programmed it and asked where the backup copy was located, but was told she didn't have time to make a backup copy. Okay, now I get to write my own code at midnight after not sleeping. I was able to re write the code and the machine actually ran better and more efficiant than before.

That same night as I was packing up my tools I was approached by an operator who was running a new element trimming machine. Thery said it was too slow and they needed to get a shipment out by morning. I timed the sequence and it took about 6 minutes to complete one cycle. The machine was running with servos and a servo can run as high as 10000 rpm. I increased the speed of the servo at the beginning of the cycle to 100 percent, then slowed down the speed to make a precision cut and then set the return speed to 100 percent.

This change decreased the time from 6 minutes per cycle to 2.5 minutes. The operator was very happy and the supervisor said now they can get the shipment out. I came in the next day to some very unhappy faces in the automation department along with my supervisor. I was told to put the program back to original because I wasn't an engineer and had no business changing the machine. I explained that production comes first, but if the engineers want the program changed, they can do it themselves. I was told they don't know how to change it back, and I was to teach them how to program a servo motor. So, I'm not qualified to make any changes but i am qualified to teach someone how to program.

I have been in demand since that day and it has been a great career. If anyone want to get into a wonderful trade and stick with it you can wright your own ticket.

Mike Lindahl

www.ingramcontent.com/pod-product-compliance
Lightning Source LLC
Chambersburg PA
CBHW070354230526
45471CB00006B/2568